NATIONAL GEOGRAPHIC

My Five Senses

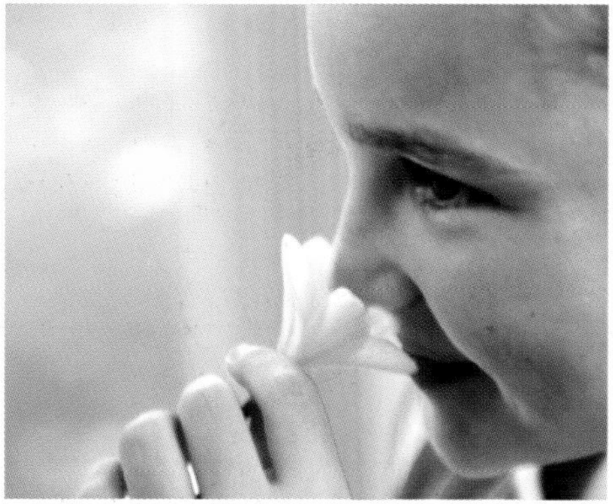

Zoe Sharp

See

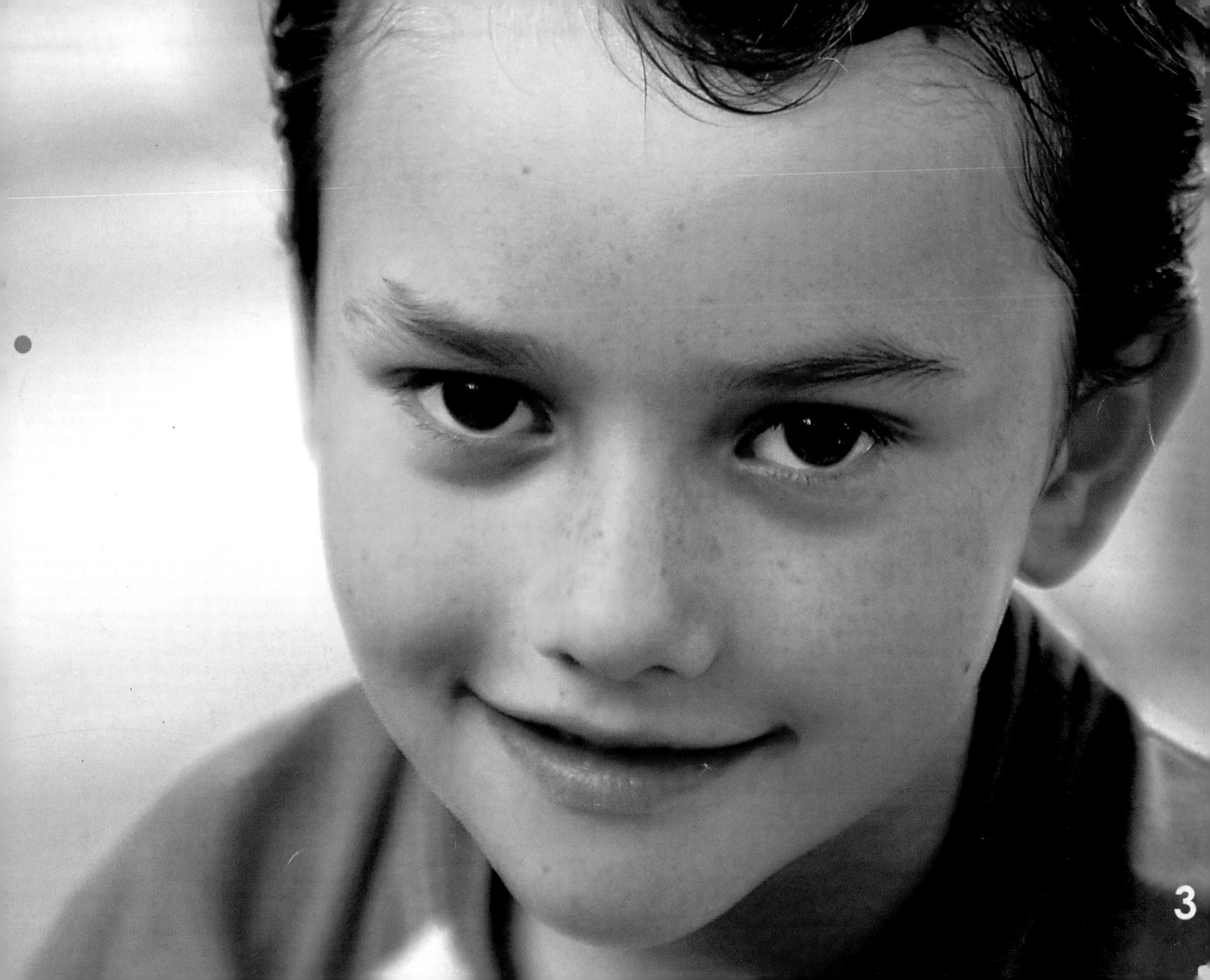

Hear

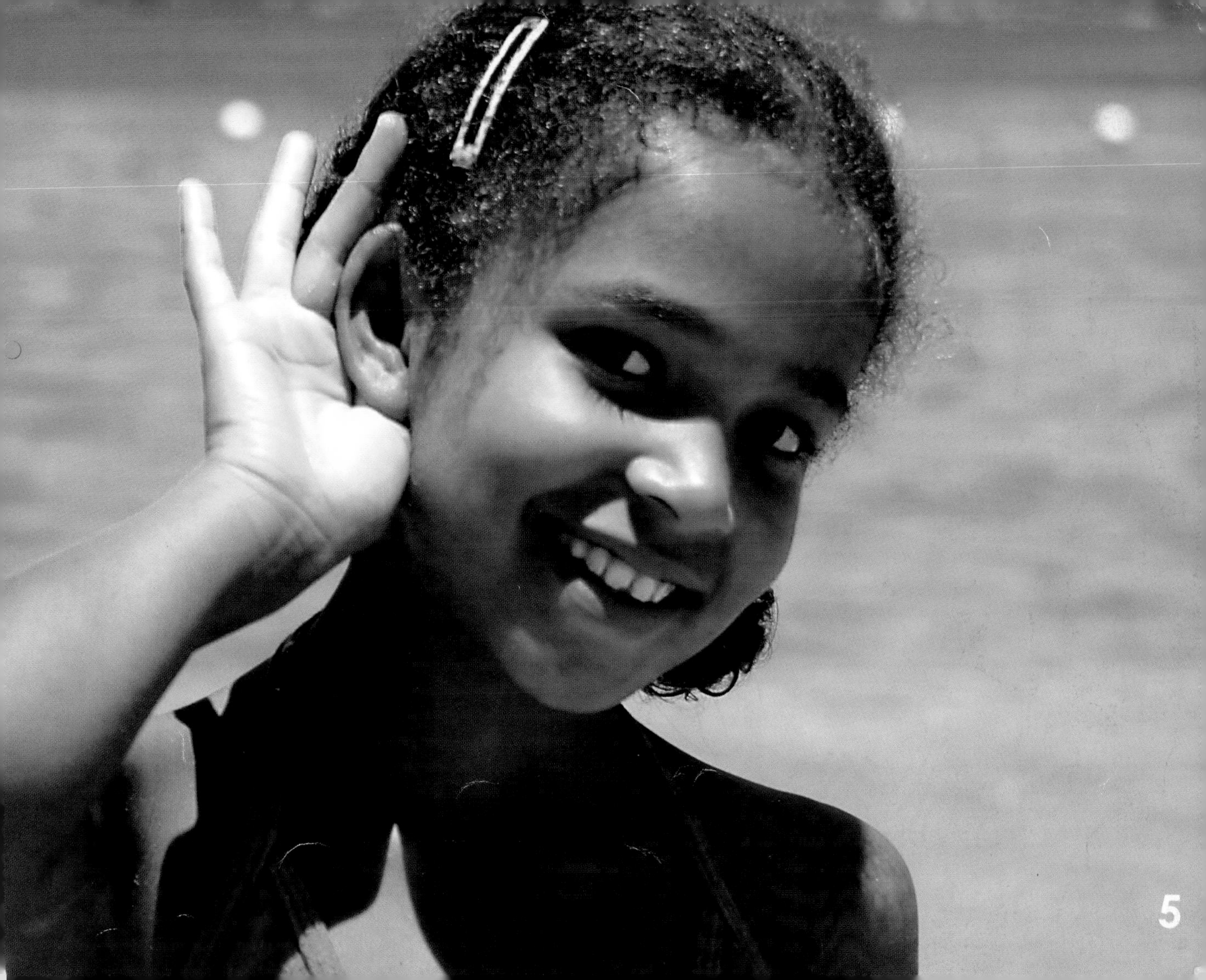

Smell

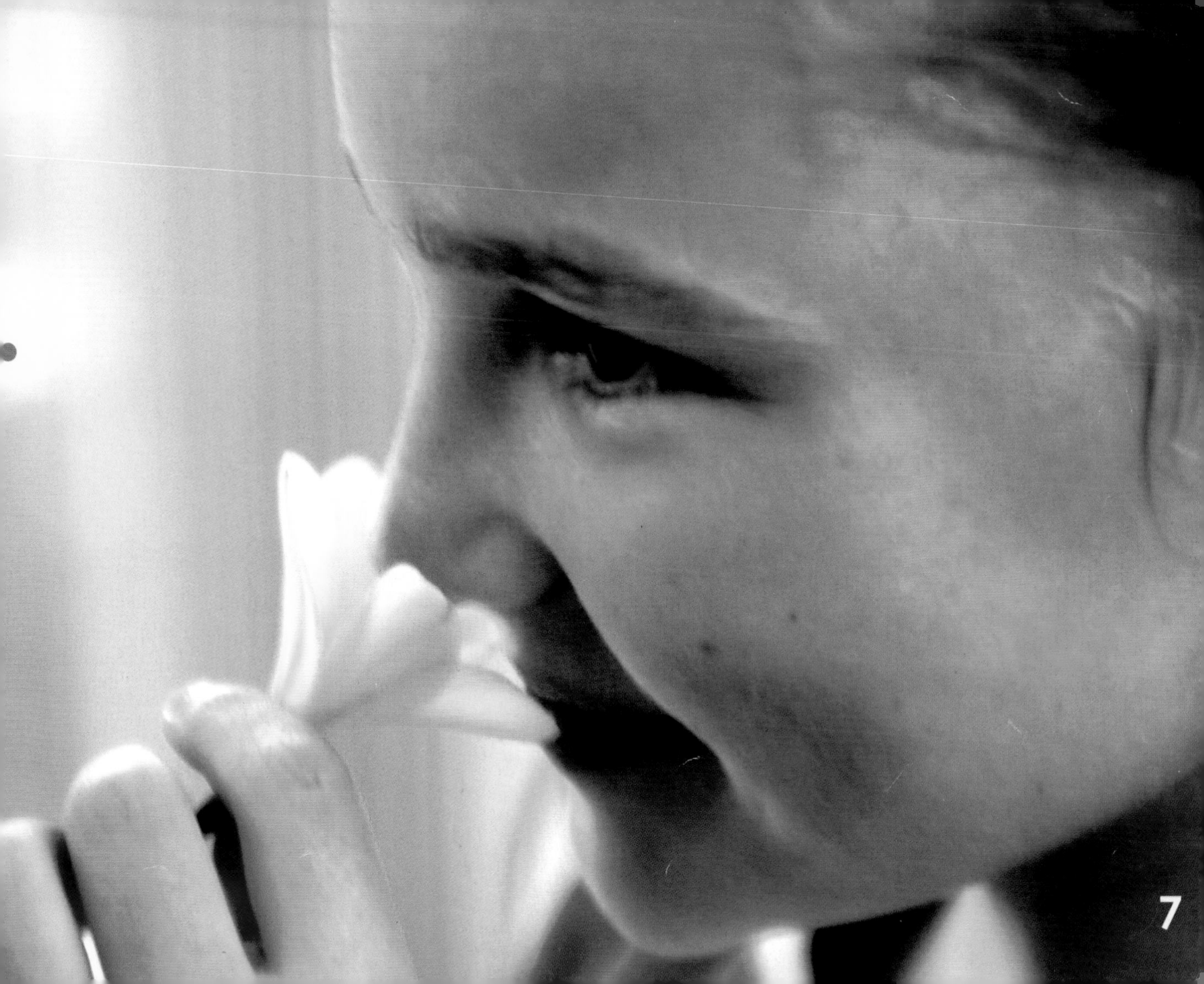

Touch

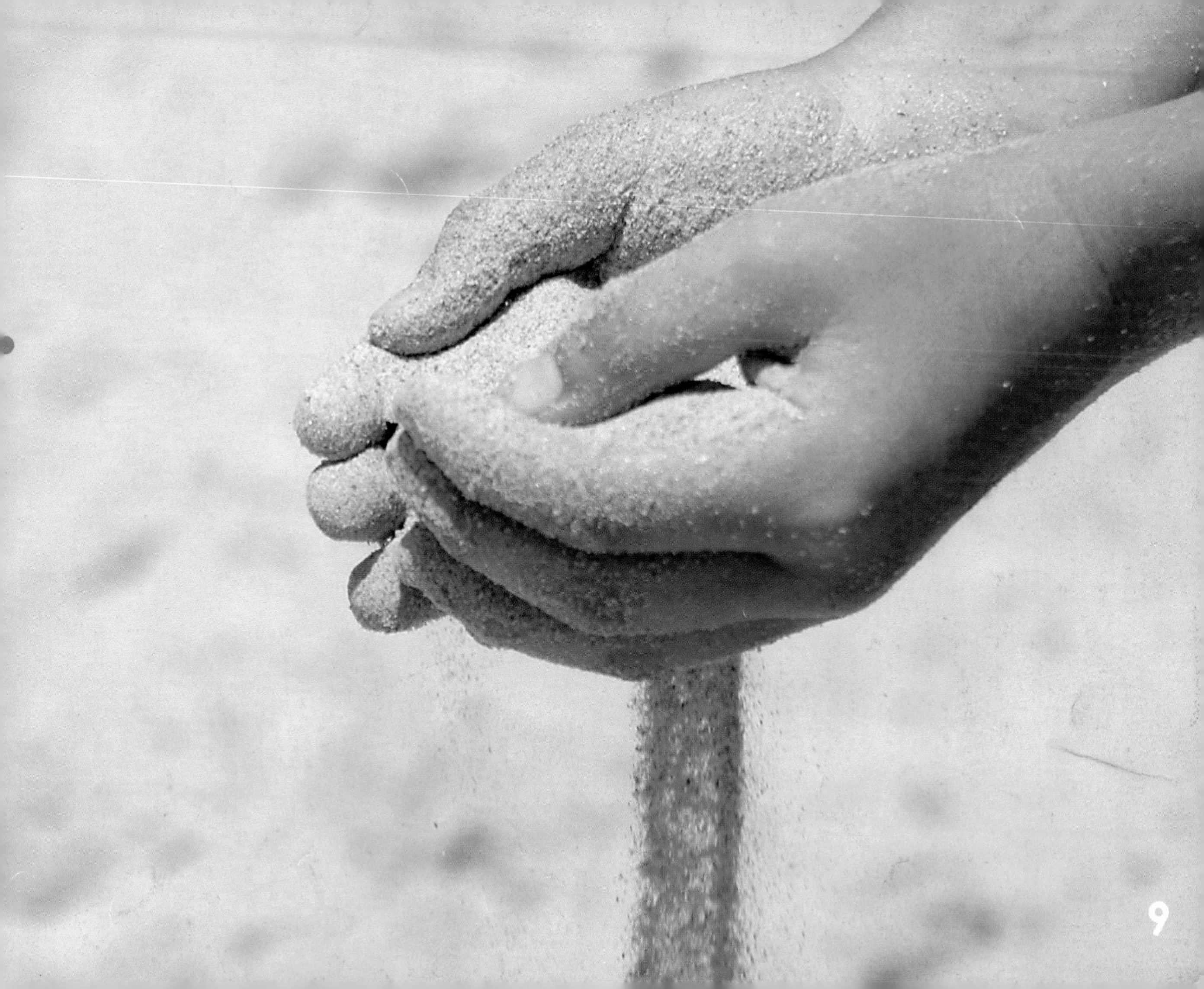

Taste

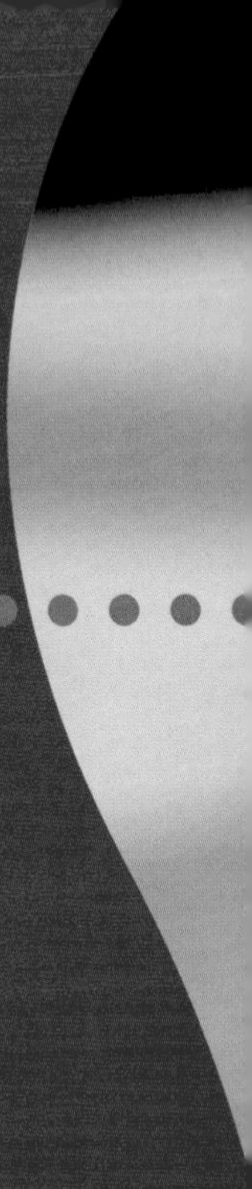

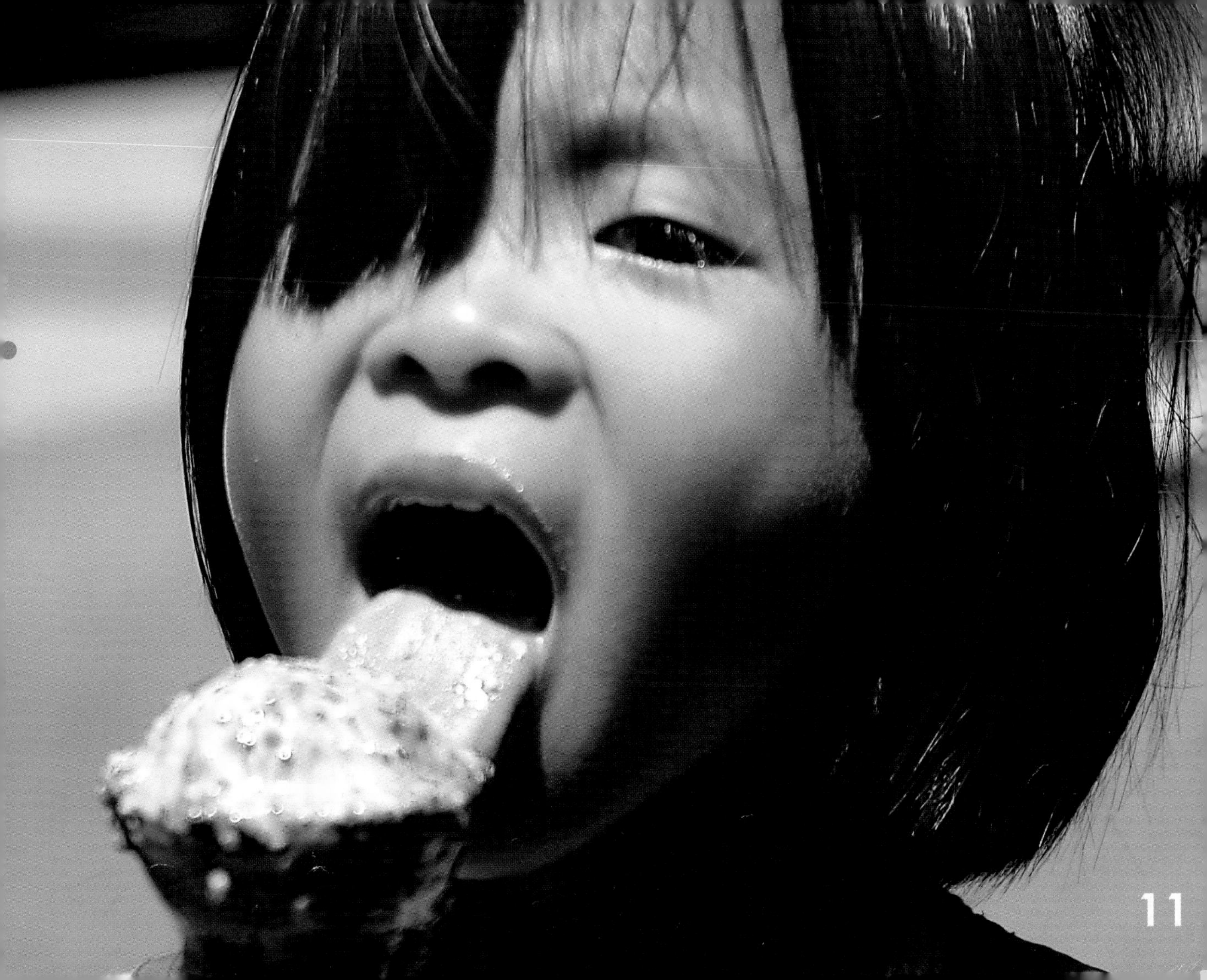

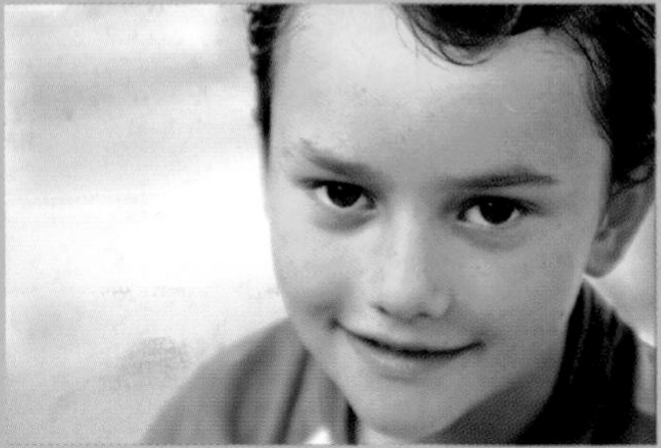

See

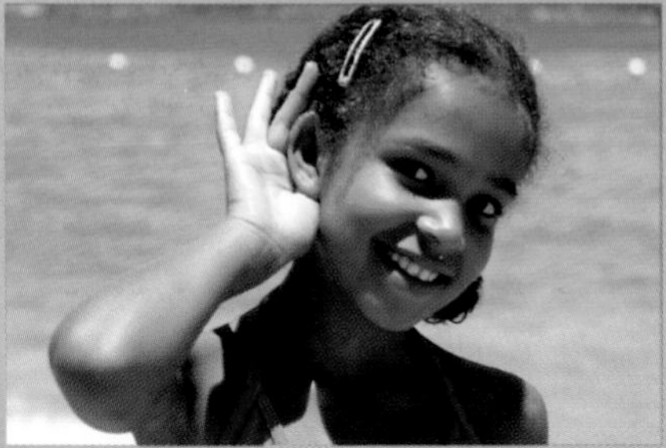

Hear

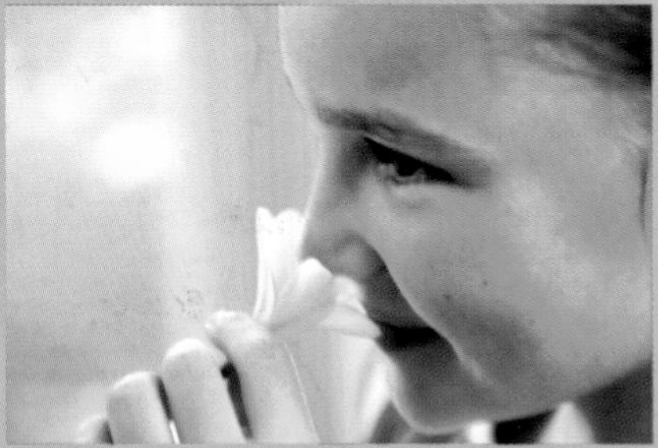

Smell

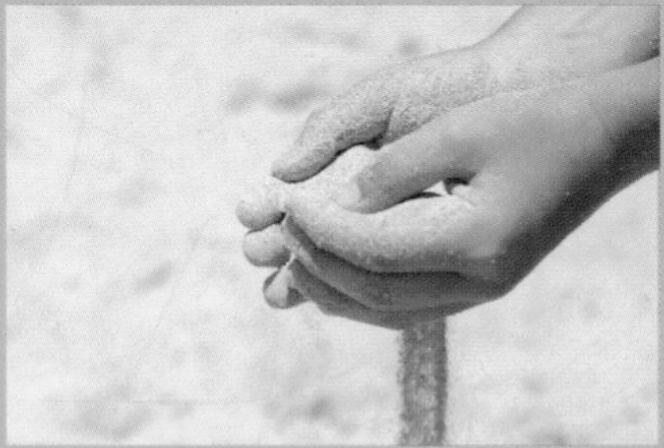

Touch

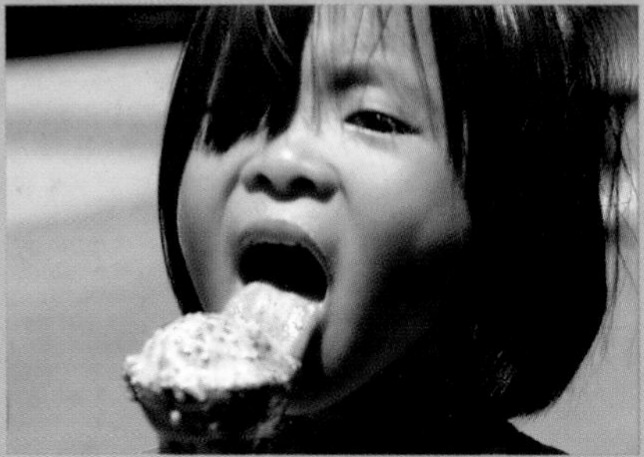

Taste